Sunkisses

LARSEE H. MAC

DEDICATION PAGE

Lord, thank you for embedding the gift of writing within me. Thanks for being the "Dream Giver" who has gifted us all. I hope that by me creating this book, it inspires others to live out their dreams too.

Thanks to my parents for always instilling the importance of education in me. I love you both dearly.

Nate- Thanks for your love and patience.

Eden- This book is only possible because of you. Thanks for allowing me to use my imagination with you!

Efe, Shannon and Robert- You all are amazing!

Thank you to the countless amount of family, friends and associates who helped make Sunkisses a reality!

It all started the day Aubrey decided to play in her backyard.

As she began to explore and discover all that spring had brought with it, she felt a crisp breeze of air rush past her face.

She couldn't help but notice the newly filled branches with the brightest green leaves.

Mesmerized by the floating dandelions soaring across the yard, Aubrey stumbled upon the most beautiful flower that she had ever seen.

Without hesitating, she reached down to pick the flower out of the ground. Just as she was about to pluck the flower, it spoke!

In a teeny, tiny voice the flower said, "Please don't pick me or I will wrinkle and crinkle, then wither away."

"Aaahhh!!!" screamed Aubrey.

Surprised that the flower could talk, Aubrey leaned in closer so she could hear it clearly.

"You see, this is my home and it gives me everything I need in order to live." Unable to resist, Aubrey reached down to pick the flower, again.

"WAIT!" Shouted the flower, much louder than before. "There are so many things that my home gives me". "If you pick me, I will surely wrinkle and crinkle, then wither away."

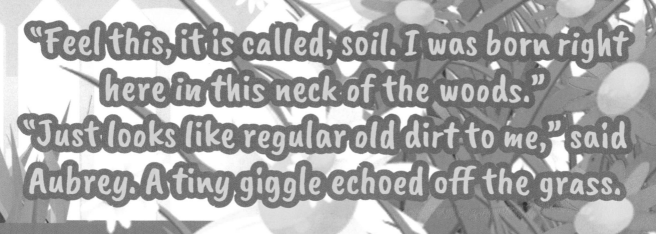

"Feel this, it is called, soil. I was born right here in this neck of the woods."
"Just looks like regular old dirt to me," said Aubrey. A tiny giggle echoed off the grass.

Right below the surface are my roots and they all fit perfectly. "What do you drink when you get thirsty?" Aubrey asked. "The morning dew and the rain we'll get this spring keeps me hydrated."

Look up there. I'd like to introduce you to my good friend, Sunny. He gives me all the nutrients I need to grow. Just then, Aubrey got an idea! "Wait here, I'll be right back."

Within seconds, Aubrey was scrambling through some materials in the shed. Clunk...Bang... Plop..."Ahh ha! Got it!"

Walking back towards the flower with a wagon filled with all sorts things, Aubrey's face glowed with excitement.

"How would you like to come home with me? We could be the best of friends and talk to each other everyday," said Aubrey.

Well, I thought you'd say that. In my wagon I have soil, water and a flower pot that will allow all of your roots to fit perfectly.

"What about my nutrients?" said the flower. "Sunny can give you all the sunkisses you need from the window sill", Aubrey thought.

"Thanks but I don't think I can do it. I will be much safer here" replied the flower.

The next couple of days Aubrey visited her new flower friend. They talked and laughed until they couldn't laugh anymore.

"On those days they would play together until the sun began to set."

Aubrey would return to her home and the flower, already comfortably in her home.

The next day, spring decided to bring an enormous amount of rain. So much that it almost drowned the flower. Aubrey quickly threw on her rain boots and jacket to go rescue her friend.

To her surprise, all the materials in her wagon were still there. She got to the flower just in time. The rushing waters had exposed most of the roots so it was easy to pull from the ground.

She placed the now muddy soil in the pot then placed the flower in. Aubrey dashed to her house with the flower pot in hand. With water dripping everywhere they looked at each other then laughed as they closed the door shut.

Thank you so much! You are such a great friend. All I need is a little sunlight and I'll be good to go. Just then as Aubrey placed the flower in her window sill, Sunny came out shining brightly for all to see.

"Ahh..this feels amazing," said the flower as the sunlight pierced through the petals and stem.

"I'm starting to think spring is my favorite season," said Aubrey. "Well I will take a rain check," said the flower.

The End

Glossary

Branches- A part of a tree that grows out from the trunk pg. 3

Dandelions- Part of the daisy family, a very common wild plant that has bright yellow flowers pg. 4

Dew -Drops of water that form outside at night on grass, trees pg. 12

Flower- The part of a plant that is often brightly colored, that usually lasts a short time, and from which the seed or fruit develops pg. 18

Kettle- A container used to hold water or liquids pg. 18

Petals- One of the soft, colorful parts of a flower pg. 27

Season One of the four periods (spring, summer, autumn, and winter) into which the year is commonly divided pg. 28

Soil- The top layer of earth in which plants grow pg. 11

Spring- The season after winter and before summer, in which vegetation begins to appear pg. 2

Stem- The main long and thin part of a plant that rises above the soil and supports the leaves and flowers pg. 27

How to Plant a Seed

Materials
- Seeds, beans usually work well
- Potting soil
- Cups or other small containers to plant the seeds
- Plain wooden stick (a paint stirrer is perfect), a piece of sturdy cardboard, or a ruler to measure plants as they grow

Preparation
- Cardboard or a piece of wood so that you can write the dates of each measurement right on the measuring tool.
- If you choose to use a ruler, you can describe the plant as "almost four inches tall" or "between 3 and 4 inches tall." Don't worry too much about exact measurements.

Directions
1. Put soil into the cups or containers.
2. Following the instructions on the seed packet, plant as many seeds as you like. (Plant at least a few in case some don't grow.) Add a little water.
3. Put the cups in a sunny spot. (A sunny window should work if it isn't quite growing season in your area. Check the seed packet for information.
4. WAIT. Growing takes time. Check the cups regularly—every day or every other day. Water the plants if the soil is dry.

5.   You might want to measure the plant. You can use a ruler or just use a plain piece of wood or cardboard. Place one end on the top of the soil and mark how tall the plant is. Write the date.

6.   Measure and record your observations of the plant regularly — once a week is good. (You'll probably need to water the plants more often.)

7.   Over a number of weeks you'll observe how the plant changes and grows. You'll also have records of the changes. Talk with children about how the plant has changed. Talk about how long it took. How many days has it been growing?

8.   Transplant the seedlings into the garden or a larger pot so that they can continue to grow.

http://www.pbs.org/parents/sid/activities/growing-plants/

Made in the USA
Middletown, DE
26 November 2022